Clever Manka

retold by Sharon Fear
●
illustrated by Mary King

MODERN CURRICULUM PRESS
Pearson Learning Group

Once there were two farmers
working a piece of land together.
They were digging and turning the
earth, when what should turn up,
but a cup made of gold! It was
from olden times, and likely very
valuable. They began to argue
about who should have it.

"My hoe touched it first," said one.

"But certainly I saw it first," said the other.

"Yes, but I pulled it out of the ground!"

"Perhaps. But I. . . . "

This went on and on, until the only thing they could agree on was that they couldn't agree. They stood there scowling at each other. Someone else would have to settle the argument.

So they put the matter before the village judge. This judge was not at all certain how to decide. At last he told the two farmers that he would ask them three riddles. The one who came back the next morning with the best answers would have the gold cup.

The judge asked, "In all the world, what is the richest thing? What is the heaviest thing? And what is the swiftest thing?"

The first farmer went home. Feeling puzzled, he thought long and hard about the three riddles.

Finally he said to himself, "Why, it's not so hard. I know just what to say."

The other farmer went home too. He also was puzzled.

Now, this man had a clever daughter named Manka. When he told her about the riddles, she thought for a while. Then she thought for a while longer. Finally she told her father what answers he should give the judge the next day.

The next day, standing before the judge, the first man gave his answers.

"In all the world," he said, "the richest thing is the king. The heaviest thing is lead. And the swiftest thing is my bay mare, which can outrun any steed in the land."

Then the second man gave his answers, those suggested by his daughter.

"In all the world," he said, "the richest thing is the Earth. For out of the Earth comes everything we need. The heaviest thing is sorrow, which, when it comes, lies upon us heavier than stone. And the swiftest thing is the mind, for it can travel around the world in an instant."

The judge was very impressed by the second man's answers. He instantly awarded the gold cup to the man.

Then the judge looked at the man. "Tell me," he said. "Did you think of those answers by yourself? Or did you have help?"

The man admitted that he had a daughter named Manka who was uncommonly clever, and that she had told him what to say.

"I would like to meet this clever Manka," said the judge. "Will you bring her here tomorrow?"

And the man said, "Yes, certainly!"

When Manka and her father appeared the next day, a trial was in progress. Two brothers had inherited a farm when their father died.

Some of this farmland was rich and some of it was quite poor. The brothers could not agree how to divide it.

"Manka!" said the judge. "I hear you are uncommonly clever. How would you settle this dispute?"

Manka thought for a while.
Then she said that she would let
one brother divide the land and let
the other brother have first choice.

The brothers were more than
happy with this decision. And so
was the judge. He was also
delighted with Manka. She was
not only clever, but also had a very
pleasing manner.

After a time it came about that the judge wanted to marry Manka, and she wanted to marry him. Manka's father was happy at the prospect. But the judge's father had objections. After all, the judge was a man of power and privilege. Manka was only the daughter of a peasant.

The young judge told his father how clever Manka was.

"Very well," said his scowling father. "If she is so clever, let her do this. Ask her to come to you neither by day nor by night, neither walking nor riding, and neither clothed nor unclothed. If she can do that, you may marry."

Manka was told of these conditions. She thought for a while. Then she said to her father, "Bring me the goat from the pasture and a long length of fish net."

Early the next morning, long before sunrise, Manka arose. She wrapped herself in the fish net. Then she jumped on the goat's back and rode along with one foot dragging on the ground.

She arrived at the judge's house just at dawn, as the stars were beginning to fade. She had come to him neither by day nor by night, neither walking nor riding, neither clothed nor unclothed.

She had done all that the judge's father asked. He had no choice but to give his permission. Only one more thing stood in the way of the wedding.

"Just promise me this," said the judge to Manka. "You must never interfere with any of my judgments. If you disobey me in this, I will send you back to your father."

Manka promised. And so they were married and lived quite happily for a time.

Then two men came to court to determine which one owned a certain colt. At the trial it came out that both men had been in the marketplace at the same time. A mare belonging to one man had given birth under the other man's wagon. Now the owner of the wagon was claiming ownership of the foal.

Perhaps the judge was tired or thinking of something else at the time. At any rate, he said, "The owner of the wagon is, of course, the owner of the colt." And that was that.

The owner of the mare was angry at the unfairness of it. But what could he do? Then he remembered. The judge's wife was known to be kind as well as wise. He went to ask Manka for her help.

Manka didn't want to interfere. She remembered her promise to her husband. But his decision had been such a bad one. And this man was so downcast that she was moved to help him.

So she told him exactly what to do and what to say. "Only you must never, ever tell the judge that I'm the one who advised you," she said to the man.

The man promised.

That afternoon he sat down by the side of the road. He was holding a fishing pole. Its line dipped into a pail of water in front of him.

When the judge walked by, he recognized the man from that day's trial. The judge asked him what he was doing.

"Fishing," said the man.

The judge burst out laughing. He said, "You can't catch a fish in a pail of water!"

"If a wagon can give birth to a foal, I can catch fish in a pail," replied the man.

Suddenly the judge turned somber. "I see what you mean," he said. "The foal will be returned to you. I will see to it."

But something about this incident made the judge suspicious. He questioned the man. Finally the man admitted that, indeed, it was Manka who had instructed him.

The judge returned home. He was very angry. "You were a peasant's daughter," he said, scowling. "I made you my wife. I gave you a life of privilege. But, Manka, you have broken our agreement. You must leave!"

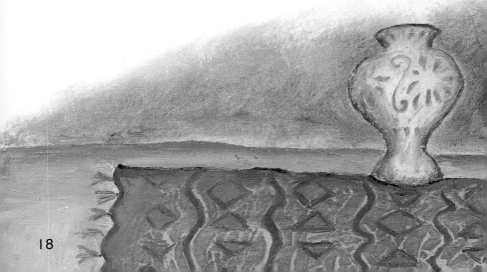

"As you wish," said Manka.
"I will leave tomorrow for my
father's house. I ask only one
favor. Let me take with me my
most beloved possession."

The judge was not a cruel man.

"You may take it, whatever it
is," he replied.

That night was to be their last night together. Manka was very quiet. Together they ate her husband's favorite food and drink. He ate little, and he still seemed quite angry.

But behind his scowling face, Manka saw sadness. And when he went to sleep, Manka looked at him. He looked so gentle and kind. Manka realized he was a good man who had made a mistake. And she knew what she had planned was right.

For Manka knew that her husband often fell into a very deep sleep.

So when some time had passed, and he was deeply asleep, she called to the servants. Together they lifted up her husband. They carried him all the way to her father's house. There they put him to bed. And then they waited.

The judge slept the whole night through. When he awoke and looked about him, he was alarmed and confused. He called for his servants. None came. Then at last he called, "Manka! Manka!" And there she was at his bedside.

"Where am I? What has happened?" he asked her.

"Oh," she said, "you are in bed in my father's house. You told me to leave, and I have done so. You told me to take with me my most beloved possession, and I have done that also."

His face went red. First it was with shame at how foolish he had been, and then with embarrassed delight. He realized that he, himself, was Manka's most beloved possession.

"Manka," said the judge. "Come home with me. It is clear that you are far wiser than I am."

Manka thought for a while. She was angry to have been ordered from her home. But she was willing to forgive her husband. From that time forward, Manka and the judge lived as happily as two people can.

Manka was as clever as always. More and more people sought her wisdom. The judge seemed to gain in stature too. Everyone said his opinions were wiser, and his rulings more sound than before.

Those who knew Manka were sure they knew why.